I0246363

Copyright © 2017 by Rhea Leto Media Group, LLC
All rights reserved.

Published By
Rhea Leto Media Group, LLC
6854 Orcutt Avenue
Long Beach, California 90805
Phone: 424.250.3773
Email: rhea@rhealeto.com
www.rhealeto.com

Cover and Interior Design By
Rhea Leto Media Group, LLC
www.RheaLeto.com

ISBN: 978-1-947185-01-2

No part of this book may be reproduced, stored in a retrieval system or transmitted in any form or by any means without the prior written permission of the publisher—except by a reviewer who may quote brief passages in a review to be printed in a newspaper, magazine or journal.

For inquires, contact the publisher.

The RLMG logo is the intellectual property and owned by Rhea Leto Media Group, LLC. This logo may not be reproduced, republished, uploaded, posted, transmitted, distributed, copied, publicly displayed or otherwise used except with written permission of Rhea Leto Media Group, LLC or unless you are a Phabb5 licensee or certified book phabb5 partner that has received written consent from Rhea Leto Media Group LLC.

Printed and Bound in the United States of America.

WHAT WE DO?
We customize and create book publishing solutions for schools, teams, neighborhoods, and companies. When it comes to our corporate clients we take the CREATIVE DNA BRAND STRANDS of your company and within 3 to 6 months we skillfully produce a literary work that best represents your company. Our job is not to simply deepen our client's brands within the community through the book development experience, but our job is to make sure your customers and clients know the stories that drive your brand.

WHY WE DO IT?
Every time you use our service we plant a student author satellite book publishing through our partnership with Publishing Hope and Branding A+ Behavior, a Student author book Publishing program (PHABB5).

To learn more about Phabb5 visit: Phabb5.org.

To learn more about RLMG and the packages we offer contact us at:
424.250.3773
rhealeto.com

People throw cards away…not books.
- CJ Miller

Eddie Swaneburg and Penske Toyota have supported WoW B since day one. They were there for Lydia when her Father died and they made sure she understood that she was more than a customer to them. She was a family member. They're a dealership you can trust. They're a dealership that treats you like family.

PENSKE
TOYOTA
A SoCal Penske Dealership

14 Years of Partnering with WoW B

Tom Mesereau pushed Lydia to believe in herself after the second March. He introduced Lydia into circles that most said she did not belong in. He's been her secret weapon and unofficial life coach.

Cynthia Covack understood Lydia's struggle when she lacked the language to put voice to her pain. She's a sister for life.

As an entrepreneur Lydia had her own balloon business, and Joker's showed her how to do business by trusting her to build her business during a time when they were economically challenged.

Plains All American showed Lydia that they cared by not only helping Wow B financially, but by personally flying down from Texas to be a part of the marches. In addition, they have been a permanent support system during holiday events for Watts families.

Through the vehicle of LocoL, Roy and Daniel taught Lydia how to be patient and kind and have a better business mind, by simply challenging her to be herself. In short, they ignored her past and loved her potential; they kept her in constant partnership with her best self. Changing Lives.

Although it wasn't in his business proposal, Keith allowed himself to be a big brother to the sons of Watts.

Pro Club was not only the first among Lydia's group of sponsors, but Pro Club has also been one of WoW B's most faithful partners. Pro Club has participated in the march every year.

14 Years of Partnering with WoW B

Sophia and Hello Giggles are like a tree of life whose roots are stationed by rivers of hope. She has managed to somehow allow her life to be a living dissertation of love, kindness, and selflessness. Sisters for life.

 HELLO GIGGLES

Heart of Compassion epitomizes the revitalization of hope through giving. When called upon by Lydia and the Women of Watts & Beyond, Pastor Eric Tietze donated two large food trucks to help WoW B feed hungry Watts families. Their support means that WoW B can reduce the number of families that go to sleep hungry at night.

Sending a loved one home to be the Lord is always difficult. What's even more difficult is doing it when your finances are low. During the genesis of Women of Watts & Beyond, Mark and Robin McKay partnered with them to ensure that hurting, financially challenged mothers could bury their sons in peace and with dignity. Thank you for years of support.

TABLE OF CONTENTS

Message from the Publisher......2

Photos......4

Lydia Friend, Founder......8

Thomas Mesereau......10

Tatti Boyd Ribeiro......12

Dr. Cynthia M. Mendenhall......14

Sophia......16

Linda Stanton......17

Sophia E. Harris......19

Janice Louis Red......21

Sharon McCall......22

Mark Anthony Adams......23

Kadeisha Corbin......25

Gabby Bradley......26

Elizabeth Dixon......27

Bambu DePistola......28

Bishop Ernest Johnson......29

Message from the Publisher:

Dear Wow B citizens, supporters, and Partners:

What would you do if you were fortunate enough to find a diamond the size of the Hollywood sign that shone like a thousand Los Angeles summer suns? Would you hide it somewhere only removing it from its place when it served your ego best? Would you sell it, hoping to capture the lifestyle of King Solomon? Or would you find a way to share it with your fellowmen?

When I met Lydia Friend, I knew Rhea Leto Media Group had found such a diamond. Lydia's commitment to healing others, repairing her community, and transforming minds through the vehicle of her Stop the Violence March, and her relentless acts of love, has positioned her as one of the brightest street lights in the city of Watts. Whether she's providing shelter and food to a family down on their luck or a hug and a smile to a person with a hole in their spirit, she never stops being the instrument of hope in the hand of love. At RLMG we believe that we are the publisher of the chosen, and it's our responsibility to partner with clients like Lydia that are changing the world through their products, service, and movement. The stories and testimonials that you are about to read are going to make your cry, smile, and laugh. Unlike, our usual fiction narratives these stories are based on real people that have had real experiences with WoW B.

We knew Lydia would be a great fit for our company because of how she responded to our belief that, "People throw business cards away, not books." Whether you're a supporter, sponsor, or recipient of the services provided by Women of Watts & Beyond you can rest assured knowing that without knowing it Lydia passed our rigorous new client intake process with flying colors. Most of the time we just say, "No. Best of luck with your marketing and branding campaign." Our motto is, "Before we can get to the paperwork, we must first discuss the people work." However, that was not the case with Lydia. Women of Watts & Beyond understands that as a company we are fiercely committed to at-risk youth, the community, and creating happy homes across the entire planet through each and every customized student, community, and corporate book brand that we make. I am proud to say that Lydia Friend embodies the "people work", and Rhea Leto Media Group is proud to have her and Women of Watts & Beyond as a client.

Founder

CJ Miller
CJ Miller
Co-Founder
Rhea Miller

Above: Lydia Friend and family, with Thomas Mesereau

"Lydia Friend is an amazing individual whose dedication, drive, and passion built Women of Watts into the compelling and dynamic organization that it is today. Thank you, Lydia and the Women of Watts, for all that you do to enrich and transform the community of Watts." - Councilman Joe Buscaino

Above: Councilman Joe Buscaino and Lydia Friend

The mothers of Watts and their children are compassionate, generous, and spiritual in their efforts to eliminate violence. They are also powerful, determined, and fierce in their desire to protect their neighborhood. - Thomas Mesereau

Above: Thomas Mesereau

Women of Watts is the mother of LocoL and the neighborhood. In my short time I have seen a peace rally that took over 103rd and brought rappers from all different sets together. I've seen clothing drives and toy drives on our LocoL parking lot. I've seen book clubs and donations that brought smiles to kid s faces. Now if that ain't impact then what is? Watts Up. - Roy Choi

Above: Roy Choi

CHAPTER 1

Lydia Denise Friend, wife, mother, entrepreneur, community activist, evangelist, and Founder of Women of Watts

Born November 28, 1959, in Los Angeles, California, Lydia is a true native of Watts. In Watts, Lydia obtained her education from preschool to high school. Lydia is a graduate of Los Angeles Trade Technical College where she studied nursing.

Growing up in Watts was not easy. It was a place of poverty for most of its residents, and Lydia's family was no exception. During her Junior High School years Lydia was caught up in drug abuse. After several years of drug use, followed by time in prison, Lydia decided this was not the life for her and that there was something better for her. She took advantage of one of the many drug rehabilitation services and began to regain control of her life. She gives many thanks to the individuals and staff of the Mary Lind Foundation for their support which put her on the path of becoming more productive in life.

First, she obtained a job to support herself and her family. Next, she married, and obtained custody of her children which were being cared for by her mother, one of the pillars of the community. Next, Lydia and her husband purchased a home in the community.

Lydia spent many years attending the church that her grandmother took her to as a little girl. After rededicating her life to God, Lydia knew that she had a mission to do in the city of Watts. It came to her one day as she was witnessing in the housing area, that something had to be done. She knew in her heart that there was something she could do to give back to her community. She realized that people in the community should live better, want better, but what did the better look like? A march! Powered by this motivation Lydia founded a nonprofit organization, Women of Watts/Taking Their Lives Back. Lydia now organizes an annual March during the month of June. The proceeds are invested into the community to help mothers with children and fathers to be good providers for their families. Ultimately, this helps them achieve a dynamic alternative to the lifestyle of self-destructive habits. The organization also offers referrals to other essential services needed by the community.

Lydia spends most of her time serving her community as the General Manager of LocoL, a community-based restaurant that believes restaurants can truly empower the communities they serve. Lydia continues to strive for the advancement of the Watts community by being fiercely dedicated to promoting economic and community development. Her goal is to educate Watts stakeholders regarding the needs and concerns of the community. She aims to employ every teen that is in High School and Community College.

Lydia's sacrificial gift of giving herself, her time, and her resources have already impacted the Watts community. And with more hard work and committed partners she is confident that her labor will continue to inspire and influence the people of Watts to regain their lives and end the vicious cycle of neglected education, crime, gangs, and poverty.

CHAPTER 2

Thomas A. Mesereau, Jr.

I have been assisting and marching with the Women of Watts for the last fourteen years. Lydia Friend is my hero.

Early in my career as a criminal defense lawyer, I learned about the scourge of gang violence in Los Angeles. Young black and brown men were being slaughtered every evening on the streets. Children were being brutally killed and traumatized. Young men were rounded up with slim evidence and sent away for life because of the tremendous prejudice against alleged "gang bangers." It was a tragedy.

A former client of mine and friend, Patrica Moore, introduced me to Lydia Friend. She was described to me as a strong, courageous, dedicated champion of her community, whom nobody could intimidate. I met with Lydia, and she asked if I would help to organize and participate in the first annual March of the Women of Watts and their children against gang violence. The motto was "Taking Back Our Streets." I agreed.

This was one of the best decisions of my life. Each year, the Women of Watts and their children march against the horror of gang violence. Each march is different from the previous one. Sometimes, we periodically stop at locations in Watts where young men have been slain. We light candles, hold hands, and pray for the departed. Other years, we choose parts of the community where drive-by shootings have terrorized the inhabitants. Again, we periodically stop the march and pray for the community. It is beautiful, touching, and meaningful.

The mothers of Watts and their children are compassionate, generous, and spiritual in their efforts to eliminate violence. They are also powerful, determined, and fierce in their desire to protect their neighborhood. Ministers and other representatives of nearby churches often participate.

A few years ago, a notorious drive-by shooting occurred in Watts. A young, misguided black man shot at the home of a Latino family and killed a little baby. As part of our March, we stood in front of the home and said prayers with the family, including the distraught mother. Black, brown, Asian, and white joined in prayer.

All of this, and much more, has been accomplished by that special person, Lydia Friend. I stood with great pride on the campus of the University of Southern California (USC) when Lydia and her colleagues graduated and earned degrees in gang intervention. It was a ceremony like no other. Here was a group of people from the streets who had survived enormous adversity and had a fierce desire to help their community. A joint project of USC and the City of Los Angeles, this program of education and involvement reflects the best in our universities and cities. It was wonderful!

Lydia, thank you for all that you do for justice, fairness, and humanity. Thank you also for being my friend.

CHAPTER 3

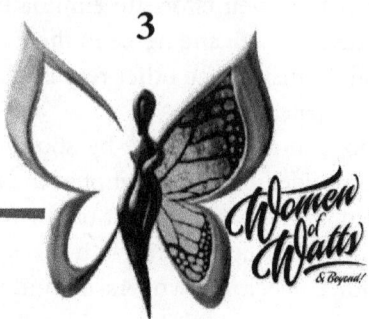

Tatti Boyd Ribeiro

WOW. Women of Watts. Women of Watts and Beyond. I'm the beyond—and recently, sometimes the Watts. I met Lydia Friend, who started Women of Watts and Beyond, where she works on 103rd Street in Watts, Los Angeles, California. Lydia intimidated and impressed me immediately. She was clearly a central force in this community, and her acceptance felt important. She was surrounded constantly by friends and family, and her work environment felt more like an extension of her social and familial environment than any other workplace I'd spent time in. That's the feeling that pervades Watts, and that entrenches LocoL, the restaurant Lydia operates. Community. Family. Friendship. And it's authentic. Once I got to speak with Lydia she became (slightly) less intimidating. She was open and listened and allowed me to be myself. She embraced me for my skills and strengths, and then put me to work. We met, and soon after I became the secretary of Women of Watts. Lydia let me into her community and let me become a part of a community that I would soon love. She is honest at her core, and honest about the work that needs to be done in Watts. Lydia doesn't pretend it's all easy, or perfect, or given. She works hard, she shows up, she fights, day in and day out. She is a matriarch. Not only for her actual family, but for her extended one as well. Whenever I call her she answers, "Hello, sister." And she means Sister. Capital S.

I have found a community and group of people through Women of Watts that I hadn't known in Los Angeles in the seven years I lived here. I remember coming to Watts in tears one morning. I thought I'd be able to pull myself together during the car ride from East LA down to Watts in time to look and feel normal. But I was wrong. I didn't look normal, my eyes were puffy and red and still wet from crying. And I certainly didn't feel normal. I was quiet and distant and rolling calls sitting on the curb away from everyone. I was talking to my family, dealing with some normal family issues, and letting myself cry. That was probably the first sign of comfort that I ignored, that I just let myself cry in the presence of all these people. Looking back, it was ultimately because I felt safe, and knew I was safe, and wouldn't be judged for being emotional. It got better for me though, because Lydia came up one, two, three, times during that thirty minute phone call to make sure I was okay. After the third time her kids interjected, "Give her some space." Lydia snapped back, "No, she doesn't give me space." And that's the truth. Like family, there are no real lines to cross. There is respect, and comfort, and being there when you need them, even if you don't know you need them. Lydia talked to me after I got off the call and gave me some tools for letting go of the stress I was feeling. I felt so seen and heard and protected that day. It epitomized what Women of Watts has given me. Strength in numbers, protection, and community.

CHAPTER 4

Dr. Cynthia M. Mendenhall, "Sista Soulja"

I was born January 26, 1962. into an abusive, physically, mentally, and emotionally traumatic lifestyle.

The bad choices I made and bad relationships had a negative impact on my life. I wanted to share some of this by saying that me and Lydia, growing up together, we fought the evil forces. Behind all the violence that was happening daily in our community, Lydia and I were hurt. After the death of my firstborn son, and her godson, Anthony Owens Jr. on August 31, 2006, we joined hands. We called a meeting at St. Francis Hospital to discuss what direction we were going after they pronounced Lil Tony dead. Lydia called it a candlelight vigil to discuss all the assaults, murder, and police brutality that broke our families apart. We talked about young blacks being subjected to long prison sentences, and we talked to different people from different neighborhoods about solutions to slow these acts of violence down. We planned a Women of Watts Peace March with all four housing developments, One Way, stakeholder organizations, CBO, and other agencies. We also decided to go back to school to get more education about our societal problems. After many meetings, the Women of Watts had committed to various trainings and certifications, such as Certification for Child Growth and Development, Facilitated and Organized Youth Programs located in the inner city communities, Opportunities for Economic Development Improvements and Individuals Self-Sufficiency Job Training, and the CORO L.A. Neighborhoods Leadership Program. Far from finishing, Lydia and I continue to serve our community the only way we know how to—by staying focused on establishing new programs for the next generation of youth by collaborating with the federal, state, county, and City of Los Angeles.

We are dedicated to just saving one child at a time. This is why we March.

CHAPTER 5

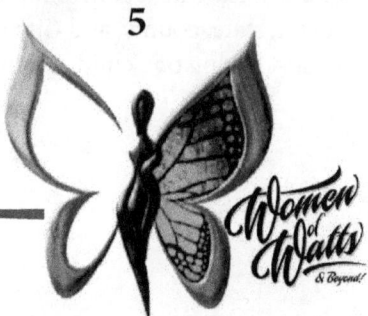

Sophia

There are a lot of people who offer help in Watts, and there are a lot of people seeking different needs in Watts—from food and shelter to counseling and day care. If you spend some time in Watts, you can see all the helping hands. Organization after organization provide donors and supporters to this community. Restaurants are often filled with social workers at lunchtime on break. Most of these organizations, however, come from the outside. Women of Watts stands out this way. Lydia and WOW are helping their community from within, and it's inspiring in so many ways. Knowing where to turn in a time of crisis or need isn't always easy or obvious. But because Lydia knows her community as well as she does, and because she is constantly building bridges and friendships, she is able to see those who need help and act as a sort of resource center. She has always been there for me whenever I've needed her. After she asked me to participate in Women of Watts and Beyond, I learned a whole new side to her operation that opened my eyes to how she connects to the women in her life. I built a company based on friendships. I am someone with many BFFs, and like me, Lydia has a collection of friends she shows up for, cares for, and who in turn are there for her. She has built her own tribe within a community that's already dependent on each other. A safe haven for women to go, to learn, to grow, and to ultimately give back when they can. It's a space I feel privileged to be in and participate in. I have found friendship and family in Lydia and in Women of Watts, a central and integral part of a place that has had a profound impact on the way I look at leadership. Watts is full of light and love, and Women of Watts is a perfect reflection of those they are helping.

CHAPTER 6

Linda Stanton

I can remember the night I met Mrs. Lydia Friend. We were on a training appointment. One of the newest representatives said she'd met her while selling purses at an outdoor market. She was nice and wanted us to meet her. I recall pulling up to her home with the intention of making a brief introduction and going right into sales 101—you know intro, presentation, then the close. Lydia invited us back to her den area, a carpeted, well-lit room with a comfortable, welcoming feeling. I could tell she was spiritual because of the way she spoke to everyone; you know, like she'd known you all your life. As we started into the presentation, she abruptly stopped us.

"You know, I'm not going to qualify for what you're selling," she said with a confidence that made us all believe she knew exactly what she was talking about.

I replied with an answer equal to her confidence that she would have to hear us out, because we were a great company that might offer a different program than what she was so confident didn't exist. She again said, "I know I not going to qualify."

She began a jaw-dropping account of how she was struck with an illness that had nearly taken her life. How the doctors had given up on her, and there was no hope. Needless to say, after she finished, we understood her faith and confidence in our Lord. Lydia had literally robbed death. After hearing her story, we knew this was going to be the start of something special. We also listen to her stories of giving back. She had started a non-profit organization called the "Women of Watts" that fed the hungry, served the hungry, and cared for children who needed it. I remember the first

Women of Watts program I attended. There were people from all walks of life. The impact of having the community representatives come together for a cause was impressive. It was educational, informative, and complete. It welcomed every member of the neighborhood. The guest speakers told life-transforming stories. I remember one young man in particular. He was abused from his youth. His story of overcoming his past to be able to speak to a crowd was life-changing. This is the kind of impact that day had for me. Women of Watts is going to be a force for change in the community today, and for days to come.

CHAPTER 7

Sophia E. Harris; Executive Director-CEO Mesereau Free Legal Clinic

I first met Lydia Friend around 2005 or 2006. My first impression of her and her organization, Women of Watts, was one of tremendous respect and gratitude. To know her personal story of tragedy to triumph, from a life of pain, losses, despair and drugs, to a life of giving back and teaching those who are mentally trapped that they can remove the physical impediments of life once they remove the shackles from their minds. To see Lydia in action when she organizes an annual March of concerned citizens to raise the awareness that the violence is real in her community, Watts, a place that most shun to visit due to its fearful aura. She invigorates and inspires her community to not depend on a handout but to do for themselves and improve their own lot in life by taking their own streets back.

Watching Lydia inspire hope in kids, young people, and those that most others look upon with disdain, is a lesson that you can rise above your circumstances, that you can rise above your past no matter how illicit it may have been. I knew when I first met her that this was a woman and an organization that I wanted to be associated with. Lydia and her organization singlehandedly assist the young Watts children by feeding them before school, because she knows from her own experience that many have gone to school with little if anything to eat. Her organization supplies youth with basic essentials for the first days of school, such as books, tools, and clothing, that help instill self-pride and self-respect. She provides job assistance and counseling to parents and to those from whom mainstream society turns their heads, as if not looking will make it not a reality.

Lydia and Women of Watts provide a holistic approach to the needs of her community and instill in each individual that freeing your mind of limitations will set you on a course of unlimited boundaries. Women of Watts is an organization worth investing time, money, and energy into teaching others that you can fly like a butterfly and be a more productive citizen, not only for Watts but in society as a whole. I am glad that we have crossed paths and will continue to assist her wherever I can.

CHAPTER 8

Janice Louis Red

I was walking through the hood going to get high when Lydia invited me into her home. She told me she used to be where I was. She explained her past, then she ask me to volunteer to pass out T-shirts for the Women of Watts Stop the Violence March. I went from passing out T-shirts to volunteering to pass out toys for Christmas, to feeding the homeless for Thanksgiving. The love that Lydia and Women of Watts showed me changed my life from homeless to living in North Hollywood, driving a new car, serving God, and raising my granddaughter. My goal is to pass on what I received—a new way of life from Lydia Friend.

CHAPTER 9

Sharon McCall

Women of Watts and Beyond came into my life October 2007 after my best friend, Derrick Kellum, and his ten year old son, Octavius Kellum, were murdered in my car. Women of Watts and Beyond helped me cope with their murder. It's a special place where individuals who are dealing with devastating, traumatic, and overwhelming experiences come together.

These ladies have shown me leadership, and now I lead. I have a nonprofit 501(c)3 for disabled veterans called Matters of the Heartfelt. My daughter Cheyenne Brown who is twenty-three years old owns an LLC business called Fun-Diggity Funnel Cakes. She completed her third year of college with a major in Business and African Studies. My youngest daughter Angel Brown, who is twenty-two years old, has an online business called Desire Accessories which has been running for three years. She is a college student completing her second year majoring in Child Development and Theatre Arts. We are entrepreneurs in our community.

Women of Watts and Beyond has empowered my daughters and me. We have a voice to be the change we want to see in our community. We go out in our community helping families—not talking about it, but being about it. Giving food, shelter, advice, and resources with love and respect. Mending broken families. Teaching chess so they can learn to make better decisions, strategize, and stay ahead of their opponents. We love our community, and we take care of our youth. Women of Watts and Beyond is an organization that cares and comforts you and your family when you need intervention and resources. We increase the peace and stop the violence so our children can live.

CHAPTER 10

Mark Anthony Adams, aka A1CREATION

My name is Anthony and I work at the restaurant LocoL Watts. I'm an ambassador for LocoL. My journey begin in 2006 when I was in prison. I needed another gateway to make a living. I did a total of sixteen years in prison. After reading an article in the LA Times giving accolades to Lydia, aka "Momma Nicey" the creator of Woman of Watts, I decided to give back to my community for all the years I worked to destroy it. I wanted to do something different, but I stumbled once again into the lure of crime and easy money. I found myself in prison again, this time for a petty crime. It's not about pointing fingers; it's about making a safe environment for our children. Women of Watts inspired me to build my relationship with the people of Watts. We're all here to live in peace. Women of Watts have parades and other events, including a concert last year.

I chose to live free from crime, I myself a victim of a drive-by shooting in 2007. I was trapped in my car, and the gunmen opened fire, shooting 38 times. I suffered five gunshot wounds. In the aftermath, I changed my life 360 degrees towards self-love. My old ways have not ruined my future. Now I'm a business owner. While working for LocoL, I have managed to be a part of something great in my neighborhood. The doors have not stopped opening. My journey is not over. Watts is my home, and I want freedom for the children here, so they can walk the streets safely. I want more jobs for the youth. My plan is to build a better mind for our youth, beginning with our own YMCA where kids can discover their talents. Women of Watts changed my mindset when they held a march against violence. We need more protection while our children come home from school. Women of Watts is a strong alliance for women. I'm hoping to give as much to my community as Women of Watts has given. I'm even inspired to write my own book as I am a poet by nature. It's another chance to share my life story, and just maybe save another life.

CHAPTER 11

Kadeisha Corbin

If I could give a summary of my life, it would be to show how a phenomenal woman of very ordinary abilities has been led by God to start a nonprofit organization by the name of Women of Watts. She has led many for over fourteen years. God has allowed her to meet many different people and bless them. In the Watts community she targets nonviolence and has been very prosperous. She now works at LocoL as a General Manager where she is very involved in the community. Her children are also involved. Two of her sons work for LocoL too. She inspired me to start my own nonprofit, KC Epilepsy & Mental Health Organization. I'm very familiar with these concerns, as I have Epilepsy and suffer from Depression and Anxiety. These elements all formulate together, and I want to educate the people. Lydia Friend has been doing a wonderful job in the community. I respect her highly. May God continue to give her many visions to bless the Watts community. God Bless.

CHAPTER 12

Gabby Bradley

As an Organizer working in the community of Watts, I have been fortunate to partner with Women of Watts and witness the important impacts they are creating. This organization, from its onset, has been determined to rise with the neighborhoods and residents to overcome challenges and grow as a community. They are pioneers for a new generation of young women, who can look to them for leadership, inclusion, and hope. Driven by sincere love for Watts, they are achieving unity, demonstrating peace, and proving that hard work and devotion is powerful enough to create the change we want to see! I am also moved to see the passion that guides Women of Watts, as examples not only for their own children but also all the children of Watts. As the First Lady Michelle Obama so eloquently stated at the Democratic National Convention of 2016, "With every word we utter, with every action we take, we know our kids are watching us. We as parents are their most important role models." These words describe what Women of Watts are so humbly achieving as they lead this movement of change. They characterize what advocacy can achieve, how celebrating the beauty of diversity in people is unifying, and how raising children as a village is the best way to protect and encourage them. Women of Watts continues to inspire me as a woman of color, but most importantly as a proud mother who wants to see strong communities and a world of justice and peace for our children.

CHAPTER 13

Elizabeth Dixon, Women of Watts Marketing Director for six years

I was introduced to Lydia Friend, the CEO of Women of Watts, through a mutual business partner six years ago. We teamed up with Lydia and Women Of Watts's "Stop the Violence" movement. I helped get supporters like Global Care, American Cancer Society, and celebrities like Katt Williams to march in the Watts neighborhood. In June 2017, we will have marched every year for fourteen years. We are expecting over 500 participants this year marching to stop the violence. These marches also provide good health information for the community. Over our fourteen years of marching in Watts, violence has decreased by 60%.

I have totally dedicated myself to Women of Watts. Lydia Friend is as real as real as you get. Lydia has inspired me by the unstoppable help she gives wholehearted to the community. Lydia is an evangelist for her church and a home care nurse for patients in her community. She feeds breakfast to school children weekly. Women of Watts helps families whose loved ones have been murdered. This Woman of God Soldier inspired me to show and give as much of myself as I can to help make a difference in stopping the violence.

CHAPTER 14

Bambu DePistola

In communities like Watts, we witness systemic attacks on black and brown men. Laws designed to target and incarcerate men in our neighborhoods are enforced by policing that is more focused on militarization than community service. This leaves an intense burden on the women in these communities.

Historically, women have carried families through extraordinary hardship. In the shadow of an upturning economy in Los Angeles, Watts is in a volatile space. A district ripe for middle-class augmentation, Watts has already seen the early scouting missions from developers looking to repurpose the neighborhoods. An increase in policing is one of the unfortunate byproducts of gentrification, and this means more men in Watts could potentially be subject to incarceration, deportation, and/or relocation.

Daughters, wives, mothers, sisters, and grandmothers of Watts—and communities whose structures mirror Watts—are left with both the financial and logistical obligation of holding the black and brown family together. As a community member, I witness firsthand the feminine energy that structures interactions between friends and family in the neighborhoods. Lydia Friend is a living example of a Watts leader, born in struggle and survived through love. A woman of faith, Lydia has been a community leader for years in Watts. I watch her navigate the foot traffic that comes through the small restaurant she helps run, sharing a joke or two with passers-by, checking in with old friends, offering free ice cream to school children, and on occasion, setting up community meetings with local activists in the store. She truly exemplifies the spirit of Watts—a true reflection of a Watts leader.

CHAPTER 15

Bishop Ernest Johnson

In 2011, I was introduced to the Women of Watts organization by Min. Bruce Jenkins, Jr, one of my co-laborers and associate pastor of Mt. Calvary Assembly Church of the Apostolic Faith. In addition, I met the fireball community activist and trail blazer, Evangelist Lydia Friend. I immediately fell in love with her vision to bring awareness to the violence that has been plaguing the Watts community since my childhood. I attended the march and also met one of her best supporters, Attorney Tom Mesereau, Jr, who has supported her efforts since its inception.

I continue to participate in this march annually, and will endeavor to bring this march to the Harbor City and Compton Communities in the near future. I cannot stop, because as a pastor, I have funeralized over 300 teens, children, and young adults who have lost their lives to meaningless and senseless killings throughout the Los Angeles County communities of Watts, South Central Los Angeles, and Compton, due to gang violence and high crime rates in the these communities. I too was blessed to survive a life-threatening event due to the grace of God while working with teens at a probation high school in the area, and therefore consider it my duty and obligation to continue to make some noise to hopefully bring some type of awareness to the youth who are committing these senseless crimes.

The march started with a child dying in the arms of Evangelist Lydia Friend, who continues with pain in her heart, tears in her eyes, yet hope in her cry, as we, the Jesus Is The Answer (JITA) Church Family, continue to cry aloud and spare not to bring awareness which will help put a dent in the young lives who are gone too soon.

Finally, it has become more than just a march but a community event that brings legal, vocational, social, economic, and communication resourses to the community where those resourses are very scarce and left by society to decay.

It's leaders like Lydia Friend who pick up the slack where the powers-that-be have failed to provide unity in the community. We and JITA will continue to stand with her and her vision, because the work is great but the laborers are few.

Women of Watts & Beyond, Notes:

Women of Watts & Beyond, Notes:

www.ingramcontent.com/pod-product-compliance
Lightning Source LLC
Chambersburg PA
CBHW031639160426
43196CB00006B/485